CRaZY NaTuRe™

Underground Animals

Marie Racanelli

PowerKiDS press™

New York

To Mom and Dad

Published in 2010 by The Rosen Publishing Group, Inc.
29 East 21st Street, New York, NY 10010

First Edition

Editor: Joanne Randolph
Book Design: Greg Tucker
Photo Researcher: Jessica Gerweck

Photo Credits: Cover Laurie Campbell/Getty Images; pp. 5, 21 Shutterstock.com; p. 7 Bob Elsdale/Getty Images; p. 9 Frank Greenaway/Getty Images; p. 11 © www.iStockphoto.com/Marcin Pawinski; pp. 12—13 © Morales/age fotostock; p. 15 © www.iStockphoto.com/Deanna Quinton Larson; p. 17 Anthony Bannister/Getty Images; p. 19 Stuart Westmorland/Getty Images.

Library of Congress Cataloging-in-Publication Data

Racanelli, Marie.
  Underground animals / Marie Racanelli. — 1st ed.
      p. cm. — (Crazy nature)
  Includes bibliographical references and index.
  ISBN 978-1-4358-9384-9 (library binding) — ISBN 978-1-4358-9860-8 (pbk.) —
ISBN 978-1-4358-9861-5 (6-pack)
  1. Burrowing animals—Juvenile literature. 2. Cave animals—Juvenile literature. I. Title.
  QL756.15.R33 2010
  590—dc22
                                    2009034734

Manufactured in the United States of America

CPSIA Compliance Information: Batch #WW10PK: For Further Information contact Rosen Publishing, New York, New York at 1-800-237-9932

Contents

A Hidden World

Animals and **insects** are all around us. When you go outside, you might see a butterfly or a bird fly past or a squirrel climb up a tree. What about the animals and insects that you do not see or hear, though? Where are they?

Some of them are likely under the ground. Many living things make their homes under ground. Some live under trees or large rocks. Some build underground **tunnels** and **burrows**, where they live and raise their young. If you dig in the soil or look under a rock, who knows what animals you might find? Let's take a look at the hidden world of underground animals!

A chipmunk peeks out of its burrow here. Chipmunks are known to gather food and store it in their burrows for winter use.

Why Underground?

Animals, like people, need food, water, and a place to live in order to **survive**. Animals who live in underground homes are sheltered from the weather and safe from many **predators**. Most predators are too large to fit inside a small animal's burrow.

A burrow or tunnel keeps animals out of the hot sun on warm days, which is very important for some animals. Earthworms, for example, breathe through their skin. The sun can dry out their skin and kill them. For this reason, earthworms spend most of their time safely under the ground. Underground homes can also keep animals warm on a cool night.

Hazel dormice spend about seven months hibernating, or in a sleeplike state, in a burrow. During the rest of the year, they live in treetops!

Underground Homes

Animals live in different kinds of underground homes. A prairie dog lives in a burrow. Snakes live in holes, caves, or under rocks. Rabbits live in **warrens**. Hardworking ants live in **anthills** that have lots of tunnels under the ground.

You likely think that birds live only in trees. Have you ever heard of a burrowing owl, though? This kind of owl likes to dig underground to make its home. Sometimes it will live in a burrow that another animal has left behind. The owl uses the burrow as a safe place in which to lay its eggs.

A burrowing owl stands on top of its burrow. Unlike other owls, the burrowing owl comes out during the day and at night.

9

Underground Food

Many animals live underground because that is where they can find the food that they like to eat, such as soil, plant **roots**, or insects. Some of these animals may also become food for other animals that share their underground home.

Earthworms live underground because they eat soil. Moles live underground, too. Guess what kind of food moles like to eat? If you guessed earthworms, then you are right. Moles will mainly eat worms, but they also eat other underground animals and insects that make their way into their underground homes.

This mole has come to the top of the ground to catch and eat this earthworm. Moles can dig up to 15 feet (5 m) in an hour with their wide front paws.

Crazy Underground Facts!

1. Juice from tree roots is all that **cicadas** eat.

2. Earthworms do not just move through the dirt without a real home. They have tunnels where they sleep during the cold winter months.

3. Moles eat their own weight in insects every day.

4. The inside of an anthill needs to be deep enough under ground to reach wet dirt. Otherwise, the ants' bodies will dry out.

5. Chipmunks hide their burrows from predators by placing leaves and sticks over the entrance hole.

6. A prairie dog is not a dog at all. It belongs to the rodent family and is often thought of as a burrowing ground squirrel.

7. Wombats save energy by staying cool inside their burrows during the heat of the day.

8. Troglobites are animals, such as eyeless spiders and millipedes, that live their whole lives in the darkest parts of caves. They cannot see but can feel tiny **vibrations**.

9. Armadillos, such as the one shown here, live in underground dens and dig in the earth for insects to eat. Armadillos are covered in bony plates. They can jump 3 feet (1 m) in the air when necessary.

10. All clams bury themselves in the sand. As they get bigger, they burrow deeper into the sand to stay away from predators.

Always Underground?

You may wonder whether underground animals ever come out of their homes. Some animals do come out, while others spend most of their lives under ground.

Moles and earthworms almost never come to the surface, or top of the ground. The desert tortoise spends 95 percent of its life in burrows. If a desert tortoise lives around 80 years, it will spend about 76 years of its life inside its home! Desert tortoise burrows can be just a bit bigger than the tortoise's shell or sometimes larger. Desert tortoises have dozens of burrows spread out around their range, or the space in which they live and look for food.

Desert tortoises leave their burrows to look for food between March and November. They hibernate for the rest of the year.

Burrowers

There are some animals, such as chipmunks, that dig burrows for shelter, but they leave their burrows often to find food. Some chipmunks make a burrow that has only one room. Other chipmunks build burrows with rooms to store food, a room to sleep in, and a room to give birth to their babies.

Aardvarks are burrowers, too. They rest in their burrows during the day and head out to look for food at night. Animals that come out at night are called nocturnal animals. Though they are mainly active at night, some aardvarks come out for a short time during the day to sun themselves!

Aardvarks have thick claws and are known to be powerful diggers. Aardvarks live in Africa and eat mainly ants and termites.

Underground Under the Sea

The sea is also home to animals that live underground. A sand dollar is a sea animal that is shaped like a large coin and feels like hard, pressed sand. This animal buries itself on the sandy seafloor to hide from predators.

A sea cucumber will burrow into the ocean floor, too. As it does this, it eats whatever bits of food that it can find in the sand or mud. A sea cucumber does not stay in its burrow all the time. It will go back inside, though, if danger is approaching. Eels are also known to live in and hunt from openings in rocks or coral reefs. Some burrow in the sand.

Sand dollars have a hard shell, called a test, that is covered in tiny spines. Sand dollars use their spines to burrow into the sand.

19

Closer Look: The Cicada

The cicada is **unique**. It has the longest underground life cycle of any insect. Some kinds of cicadas live underground for up to 17 years!

A female cicada generally lays her eggs on a small branch. When the eggs break open, the newborn cicadas, or nymphs, fall to the ground and dig burrows for themselves. The nymphs stay in these burrows for anywhere from 2 to 5 years or 13 to 17 years, depending on what kind of cicada they are. During this time, the nymphs drink watery matter from tree roots. When they are ready, they dig to the surface and come out. Then, they shed their skin, **mate**, lay eggs, and die.

This cicada has just come out of the ground and will soon shed its skin and become an adult. Once they become adults, cicadas live for about one month.

21

Underground Helpers

Some people think burrowing animals, such as moles and prairie dogs, are pests. On farms, horses can fall into burrow openings and hurt their legs. Running into mounds of dirt or burrows can hurt farm machinery, too. Even so, some of these underground animals have many positive effects. Soil is made better by the digging of animals and also by their droppings. Some underground animals also eat insects that might otherwise hurt many of our crops.

Next time you are outside look closely at the ground around you. Do you see signs of any underground homes? There is a whole underground world of animals beneath your feet!

Glossary

aardvarks (AHRD-vahrks) Burrowing African animals.

anthills (ANT-hilz) Mounds made by ants as they remove sand from underground tunnels.

burrows (BUR-ohz) Holes animals dig in the ground as shelters.

cicadas (suh-KAY-duhz) Large insects that make loud sounds.

insects (IN-sekts) Small animals that often have six legs and wings.

mate (MAYT) To come together to make babies.

predators (PREH-duh-terz) Animals that kill other animals for food.

roots (ROOTS) The parts of plants or trees that are underground.

survive (sur-VYV) To continue to live.

tunnels (TUH-nelz) Passages under or through something, such as earth.

unique (yoo-NEEK) One of a kind.

vibrations (vy-BRAY-shunz) Fast movements up and down or back and forth.

warrens (WAWR-enz) Rabbit holes.

Index

Web Sites

Due to the changing nature of Internet links, PowerKids Press has developed an online list of Web sites related to the subject of this book. This site is updated regularly. Please use this link to access the list:

www.powerkidslinks.com/cnature/underg/

24